Practice Test 1 for the CogAT® - Form 7 (Cognitive Abilities Test®)

Grade 2

By Smart Cookie Ink

COPYRIGHT 2011

Printed in the United States of America.

INTRODUCTION

The *Cognitive Abilities Test®* (*CogAT®*) measures a student's reasoning and problem solving abilities using Verbal, Quantitative and Figurative approaches.

This test is administered to K–12 school children as a means to identify potentially gifted children for placement in accelerated learning programs. A good score on the CogAT® qualifies a child for superior educational programs within public and private schools.

Analytical reasoning and problem solving are seldom part of the standard school curriculum. Most children appear for the CogAT® without a clear understanding of what is expected of them. Sometimes even the brightest of young minds can be rattled because of unfamiliarity with the questions and test format. They are forced to respond reflexively in the absence of a test taking strategy.

Schools suggest a good night's sleep and a healthy breakfast as adequate preparation – as well-intended as this advice may be, it just won't cut it in this increasingly competitive environment.

Help your child perform at his or her best AND ensure that his or her true potential is fairly and accurately evaluated!

With this in mind, we have designed this book with a specific purpose: to hone your child's analytical reasoning and problem solving abilities that the Grade 2 CogAT® test demands.

This book covers one full length Level 8 practice test that can be administered to Grade 2 students.

The practice test that this book offers will
➢ Help tune your child's mind to think critically
➢ Provide varied exercises in all the areas of reasoning that the test considers:
- **Verbal**
  (Picture Analogies, Sentence Completion & Picture Classification)
- **Quantitative**
  (Number Analogies, Number Puzzles & Number Series)
- **Figurative**
  (Figure Matrices, Paper Folding & Figure Classification)

➢ **Familiarize your child with the format of the test.**
In addition, the book also offers,
➢ **Important test taking tips and strategies**

Now, get ready to ace this test!

TABLE OF CONTENTS

TIPS FOR THE TESTERS

• A GOOD NIGHT'S SLEEP & A HEALTHY BREAKFAST!

The test is spread over 2 to 5 days in most school districts. Make sure you get a good night's sleep and eat a healthy breakfast and arrive to school on time on these important days of testing. A calm mind is usually able to think significantly better!

• I said "LISTEN!"

Listen to the instructions given to you during the examination. You will be given instructions on how to fill the test forms. Be sure to follow these instructions. You do not want to compromise your test score because you filled in the answers incorrectly or in the wrong section!

As you already may know, the CogAT® test is divided into multiple sections. You will be provided with directions at the start of each section. The directions will explain the section and tell you how the questions in it should be answered. Pay attention even though you may be familiar with the test format.

Sometimes, the questions within each section may be read to you instead of it being provided in written form. If the questions are being read to you, please focus and listen carefully! They will not be repeated. It is important that you pay close attention to the reversing effect of negative words (like not) or prefixes (like un-).

• WHAT IS IN YOUR MIND'S EYE?

Before looking at the answers, it might help if you try to first solve the question in your mind. This approach works well especially for Quantitative sections.

<Cont'd>

• EVALUATE ALL ANSWER CHOICES!

Evaluate all answer choices and always choose the one right answer which BEST answers the question. Remember, sometimes the best available answer might not be the most ideal answer or the answer in your mind's eye. You are just choosing the best of the lot!

• SLASH THE TRASH!

If you can eliminate one or two obviously wrong answer choices at the first glance, you can focus on picking the correct answer from among the remaining choices.

• TAKE A GUESS!

CogAT® test scores are calculated based on the number of right answers. It is best to answer all questions rather than leave them blank. If after 'slashing the trash', you do not know the correct answer, guess from the available 'maybe' answers.

• COLOR THE BUBBLE!

It is important to know how to color the bubble. Sometimes, you may be given a bubble test form. At other times, you may have to color the bubbles just below the answer choices within the question paper. Practice coloring bubbles and using a sample bubble test form. Also remember to color only one bubble per question.

Practice Test 1
for the CogAT® - Form 7

Cognitive Abilities Test®

Level 8 (Grade 2)

PICTURE ANALOGIES

In the matrix given to you, determine the relationship between the top 2 pictures.

Pick a picture that completes the matrix in such a way that the bottom pair has the same relationship as the top pair. Color the bubble under your choice.

1.

(a)

(b)

(c)

2.

(a)

(b)

(c)

3.

(a)

(b)

(c)

4.

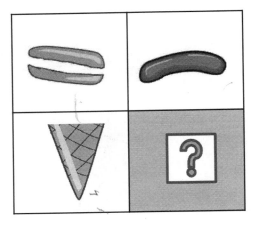

(a)

(b)

(c)

5.

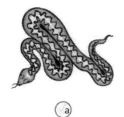

(a)

(b)

(c)

6.

(a)

(b)

(c)

7.

   (a)

   (b)

(c)

8.

   (a)

   (b)

   (c)

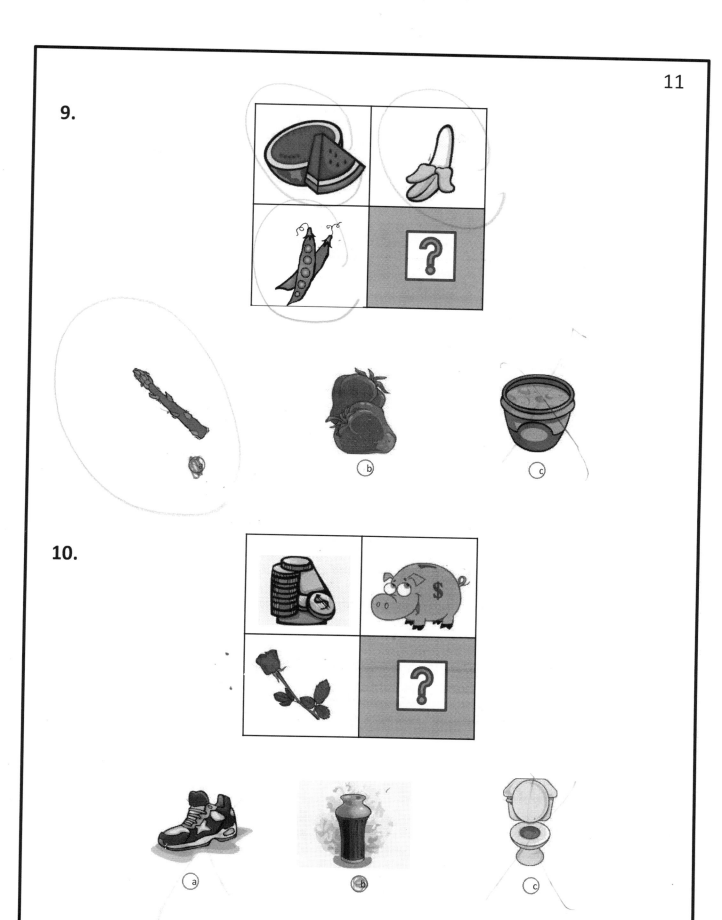

9.

10.

11.

a   b   c

12.

a   b   c

13.

(a) (b) (c)

14.

(a) (b) (c)

15.

(a)

(b)

(c)

16.

(a)

(b)

(c)

17.

(a)

(b)

(c)

18.

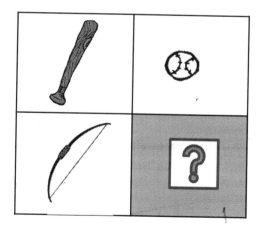

(a)

(b)

(c)

SENTENCE COMPLETION

Pick the picture that best answers the question by coloring the bubble under it.

NOTE –

In the actual test, the questions will not be provided to you in written form. All questions in this section will be read to you. So, please focus and listen carefully as each question is read to you so that you may choose an answer. The questions may be read to you only once.

It is also important that you pay close attention to the reversing effect of negative words (such as 'not') or prefixes (such as 'un-').

1. Which one of these would you use to open a locked door?

                    b   c

2. Which one of these vehicles will most likely carry a very sick person to the hospital?

     a   b   c

3. Which one of these can be used to cut wood?

     a   b   c

4. Which one of these pictures shows a mouse on the cheese?

a   b

5. Which of the following can hold the most volume for a liquid?

b   c

6. Which one of these pictures is not a pair?

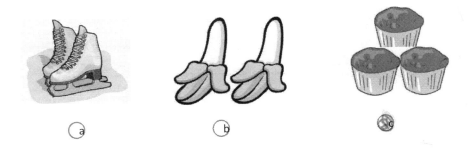

a   b   c

7. Which one of these would you use to measure the height of a cup?

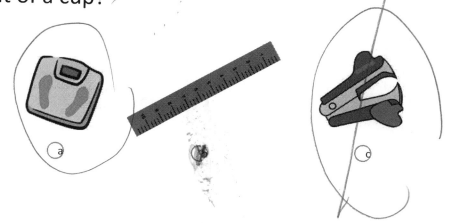

8. Which one of these pictures below shows a quarter?.

9. Mr.Wu told Joe, "I think you need to tune it before you play it" What was Joe doing at that time?

10. Ms.Carla said I had to eat my oatmeal, do my homework and practice piano before I could go biking. I am done with my homework and piano practice. Which one of these pictures show what else I must do before I can go biking?

a   b   c

11. Which one of these pictures shows an apple in between a pineapple and a banana?

a   b   c

12. Which one of these pictures below shows something that is non-living?

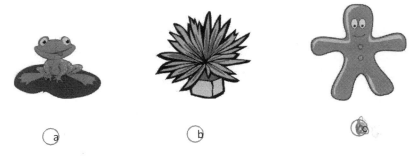

a   b   c

13. Which one of these is a 'high-rise' building?

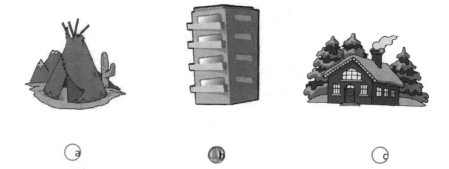

   a   b   c

14. Peter helped his dad wash the car. Which one of these pictures shows what Peter was doing?

   a   b   c

15. Maya and her mom went to the butcher. Which one of these will she not see there?

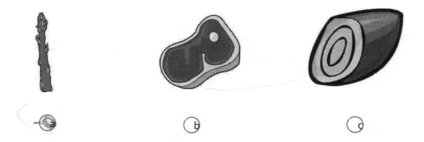

   a   b   c

16. Mary wants to make a banana milkshake. Which one of these will she not need?

a

b

c

17. Which one of these is a speedometer?

a

b

c

18. Which one of these is a mammal?

a

b

c

PICTURE CLASSIFICATION

Look at the top 3 pictures and determine how they are similar.

In the bottom row, color the bubble under the picture that is most similar to the top 3.

1.

(a) (b)

2.

(a) (b) (c)

3.

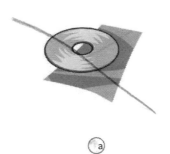

a   b   

4.

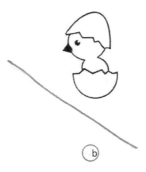

a   b   c

5.

(a)   (b) (c)

6.

(a)   (b) (c)

7.

 a b c

8.

 a b c

9.

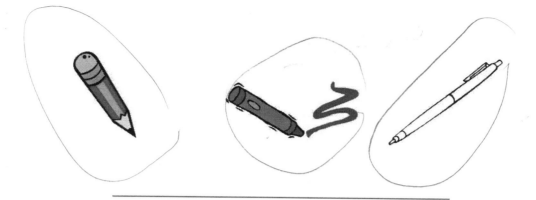

(a)   (b)   (c)

10.

(a)   (b)   (c)

11.

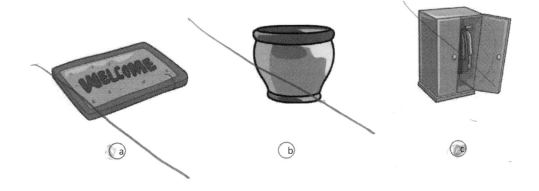

  a

 b

 c

12.

 a

  b

  c

13.

(a)

(b)

(c)

14.

(a)

(b)

(c)

15.

16.

17.

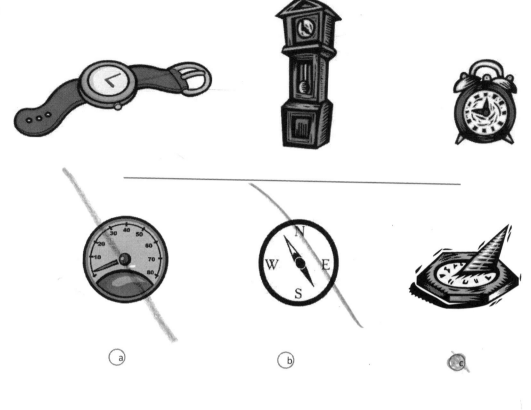

a   b   c

18.

a   b   c

NUMBER ANALOGIES

In the matrix given to you, determine the relationship between the top 2 pictures.

Pick a picture that completes the matrix in such a way that the bottom pair has the same relationship as the top pair. Color the bubble under your choice.

1.

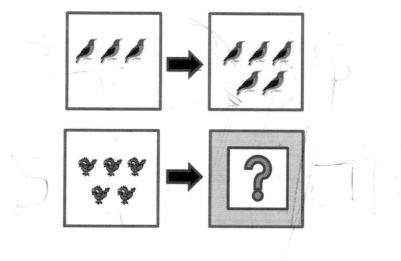

a   b   c

2.

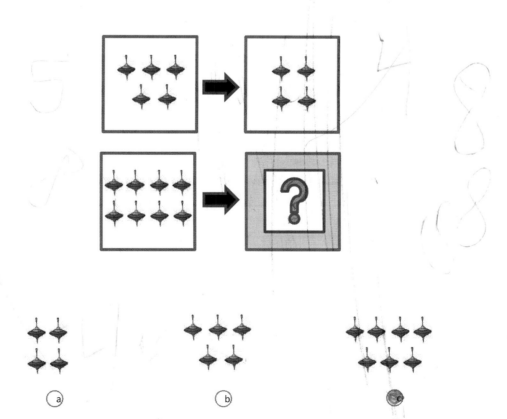

a   b   c

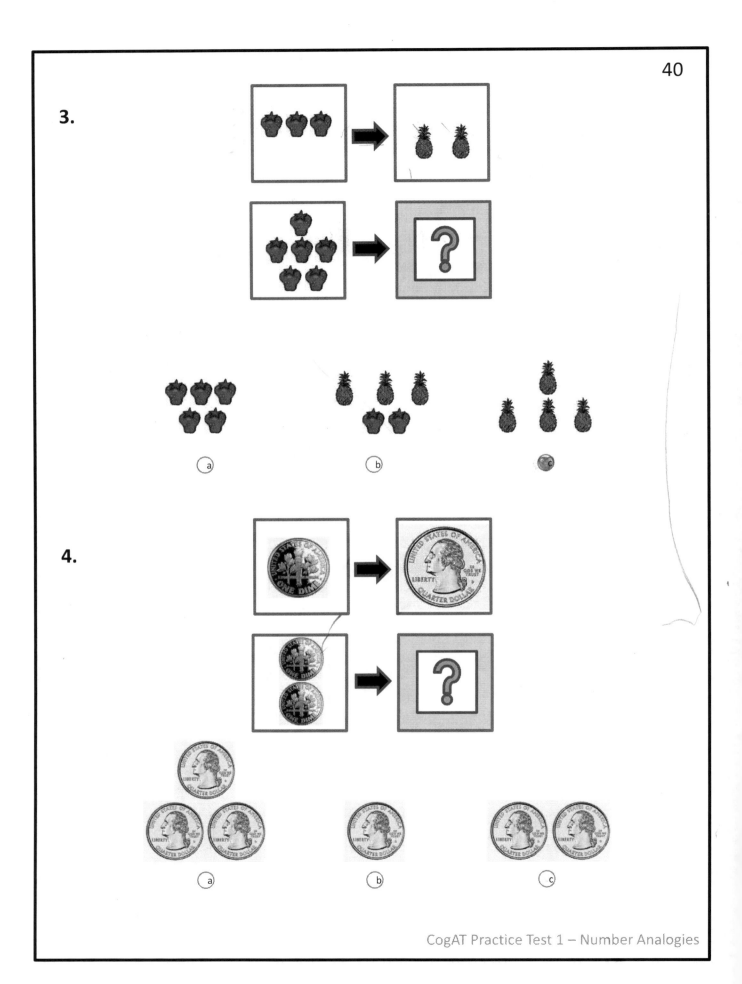

3.

4.

5.

1/2

?

1/2	2/2	1/4
	b	c

6.

[clocks]

?

 |  | [clock]

a | b | c

7.

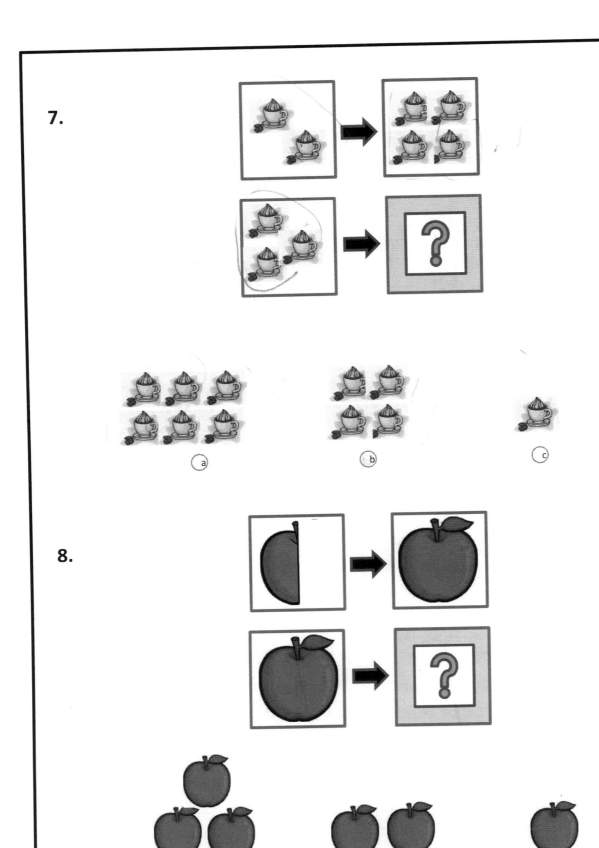

8.

9.

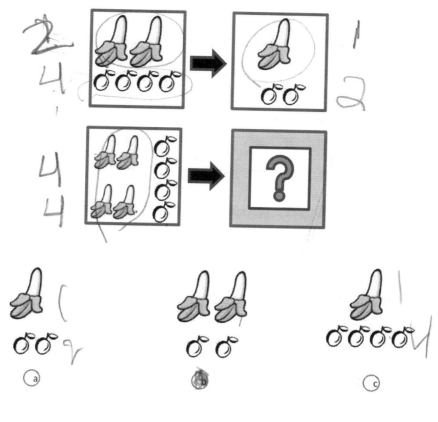

ⓐ   ⓑ   ⓒ

10.

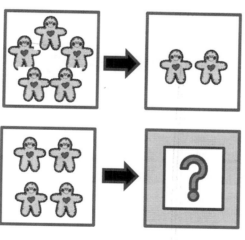

ⓐ   ⓑ   ⓒ

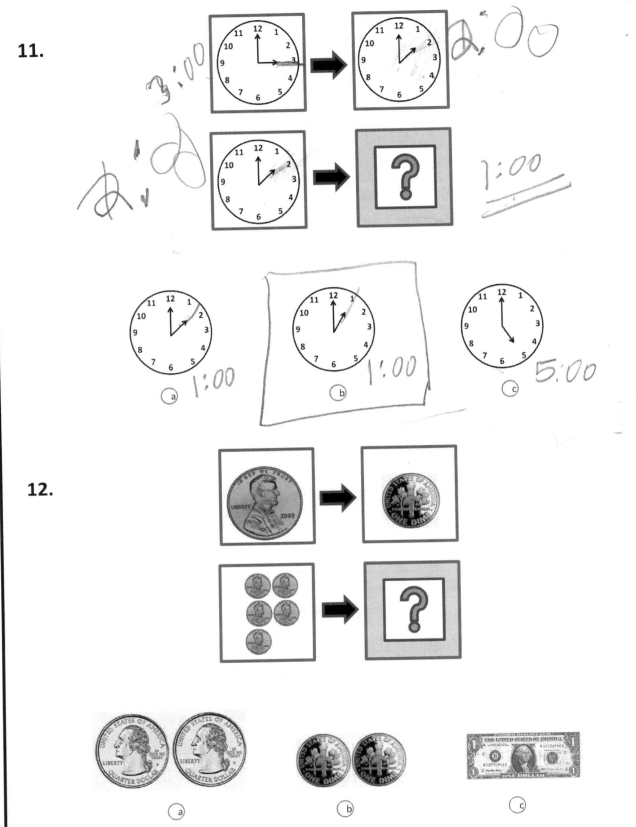

11.

12.

13.

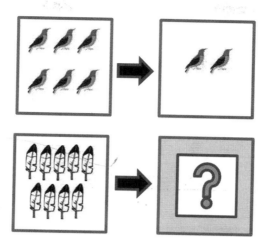

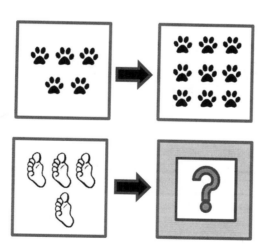

a

b

c

14.

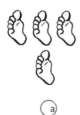
a

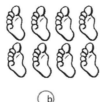
b

c

15.

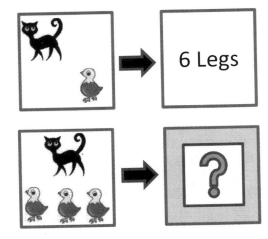

8 Legs

(a)

6 Legs

(b)

10 Legs

(c)

16.

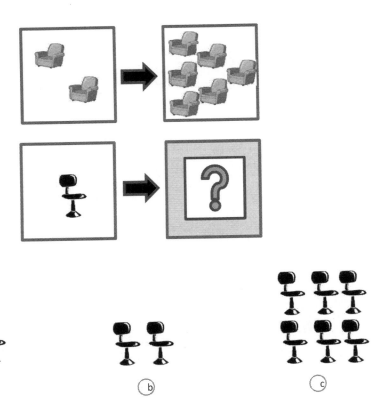

(a)   (b)   (c)

17.

(a)

(b)

(c)

18.

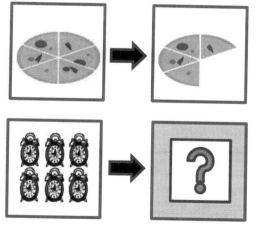

(a)

(b)

(c)

NUMBER PUZZLES

In this section, you will see two trains for each question — one on the right and one on the left. The trains may or may not have the same number of train cars. There may be empty train cars as well.

Your job is to make sure that the trains on either side of each question carry the same load. You should pick the train car from the answer choices that can replace the train car with the question mark so that both the trains carry the same load.

Color the bubble under your choice.

1.

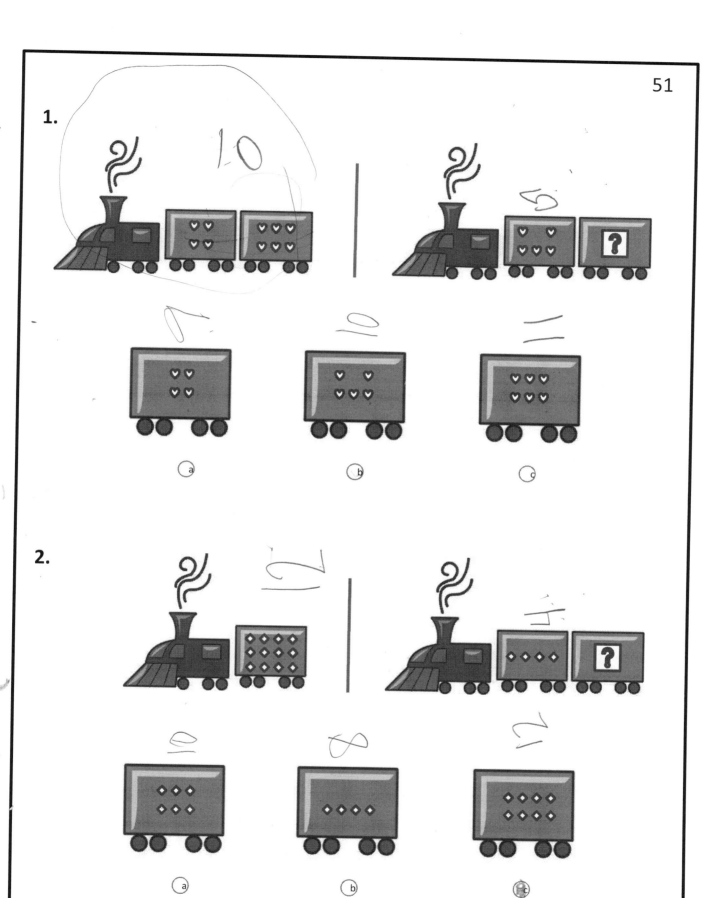

3.

      a   b   c

4.

      a   b   c

5.

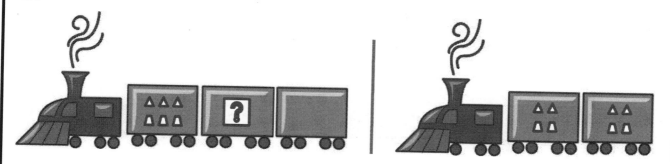

a   b   c

6.

a   b   c

53

7.

(a)   (b)   (c)

8.

(a)   (b)   (c)

9.

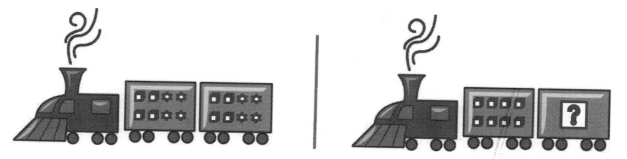

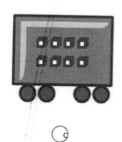

a   b   c

10.

a   b   c

11.

a   b   c

12

 a   b   c

13.

a

b

c

14

a

b

NUMBER SERIES

The number of beads in the rods of the abacus for each question follows some type of pattern.

Pick the answer choice that completes or fits in as the missing rod (denoted by the question mark) in the abacus pattern. Color the bubble under your choice.

1.

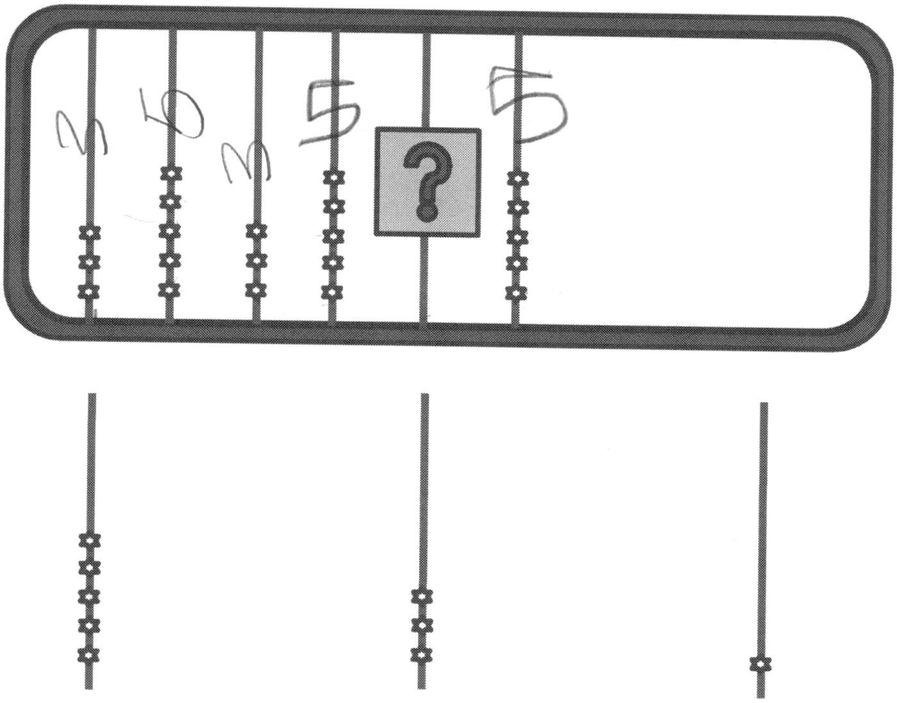

ⓐ   ⓑ   ⓒ

2.

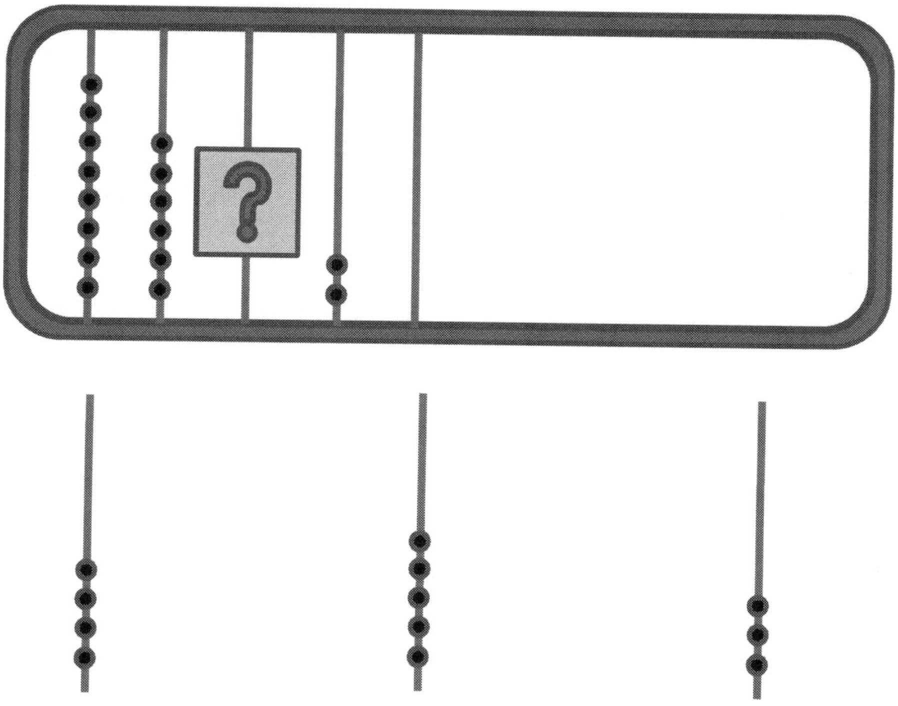

ⓐ   ⓑ   ⓒ

3.

a   b   c

4.

a   b   c

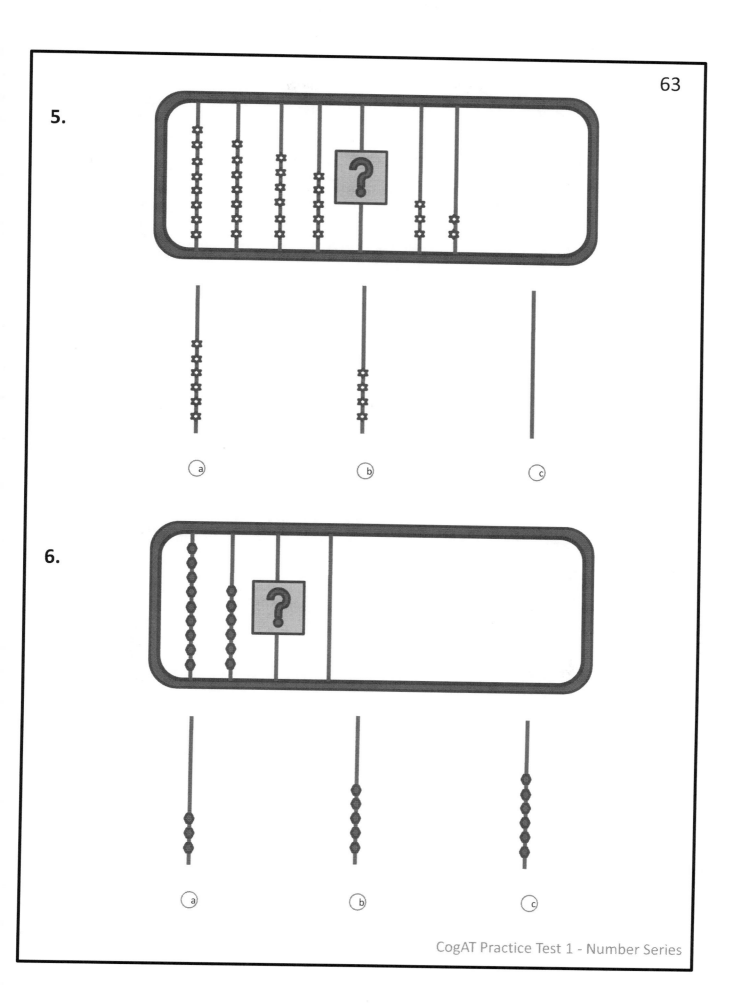

5.

a b c

6.

a b c

7.

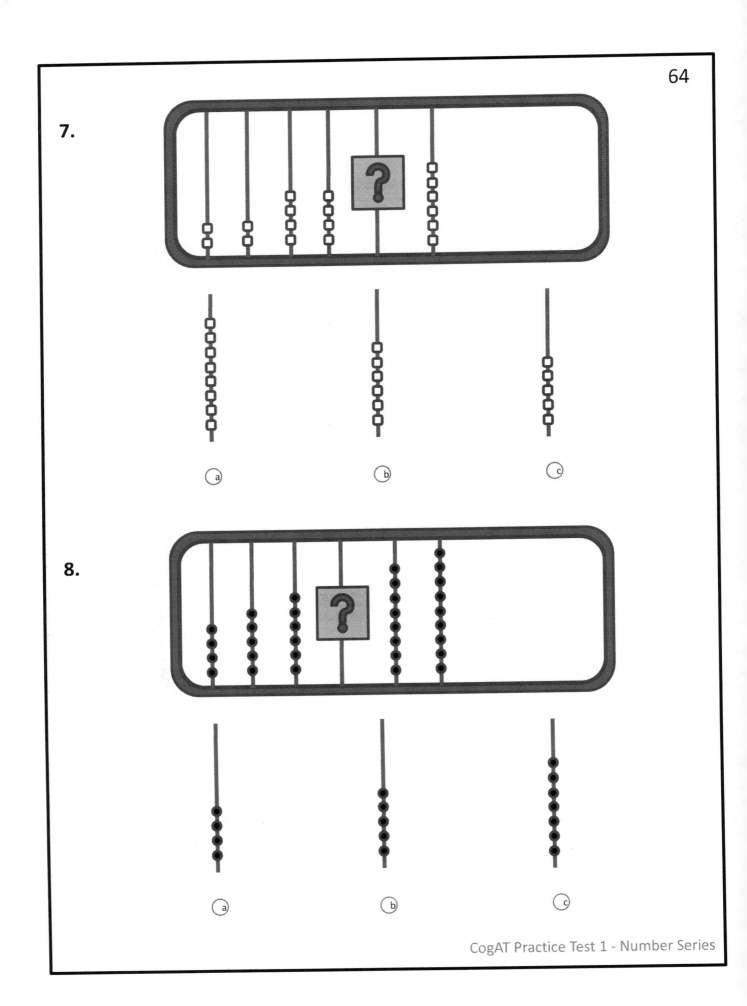

a b c

8.

a b c

64

9.

a   b   c

10.

a   b   c

11.

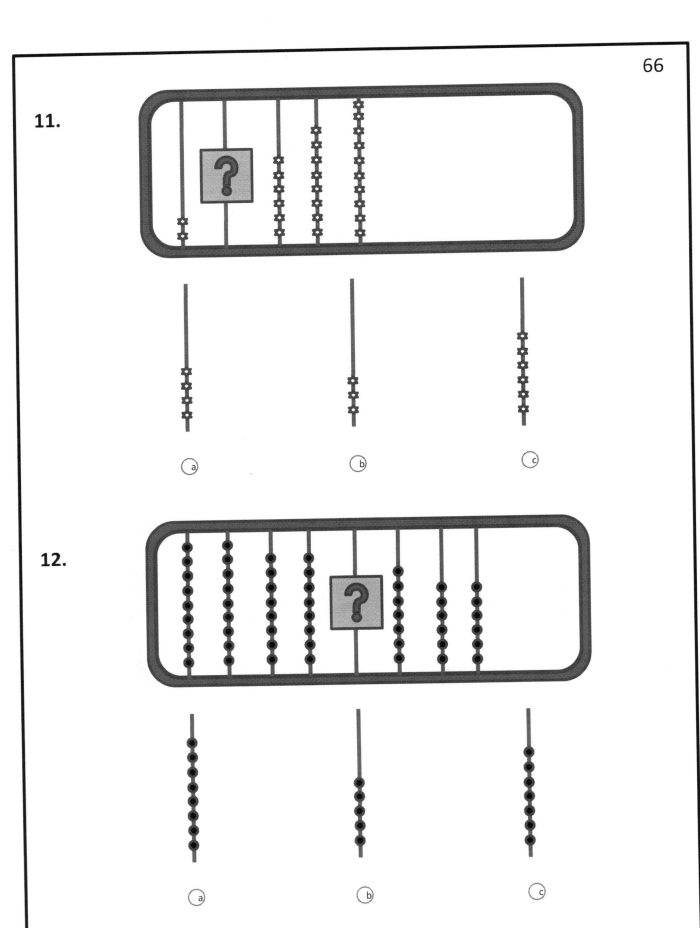

a   b   c

12.

a   b   c

13.

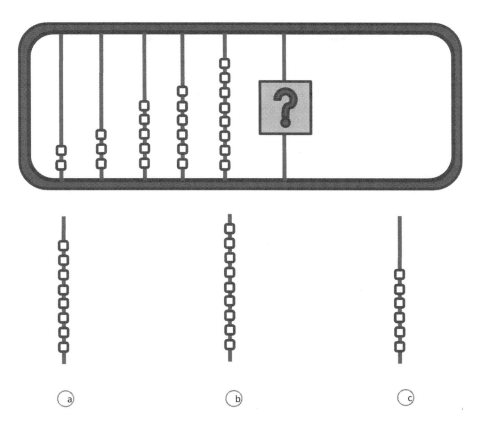

(a)   (b)   (c)

14.

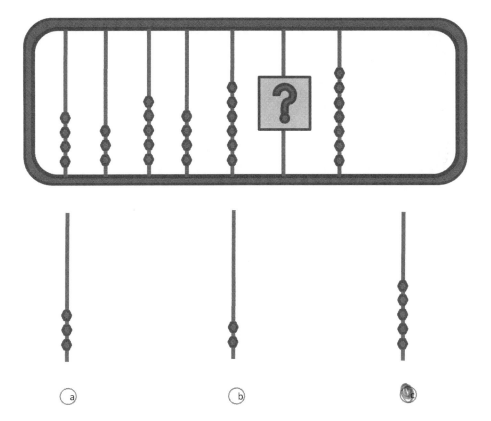

(a)   (b)   (c)

15.

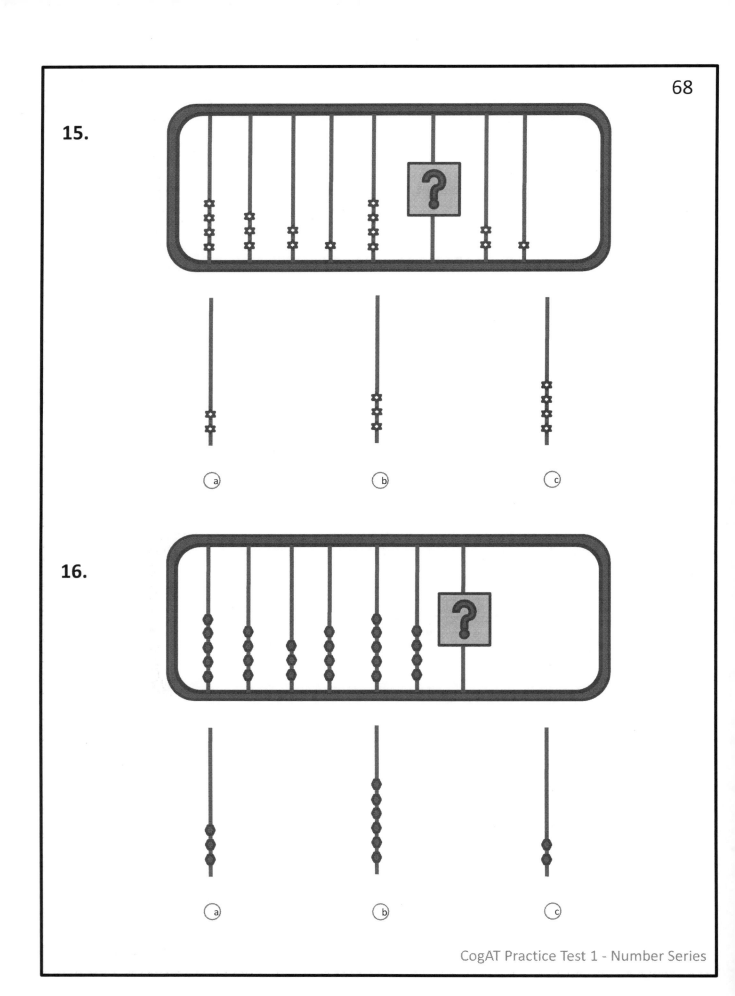

16.

17.

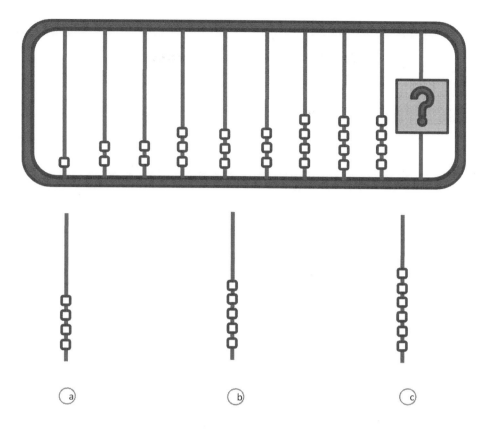

     (a)   (b)   (c)

18.

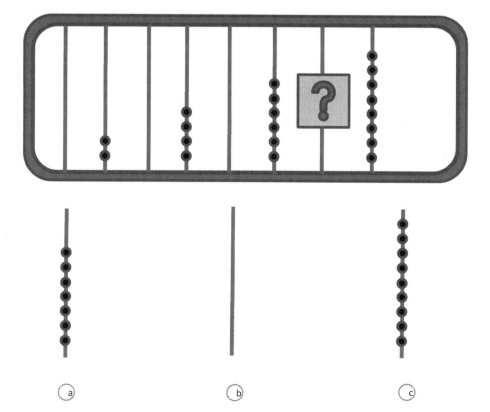

     (a)   (b)   (c)

FIGURE MATRICES

In the matrix given to you, determine the relationship between the top 2 pictures.

Pick a picture that completes the matrix in such a way that the bottom pair has the same relationship as the top pair. Color the bubble under your choice.

1.

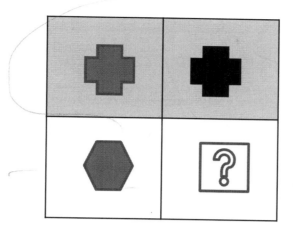

(a)　　　(b)　　　(c)　　　(d)　　　(e)

2.

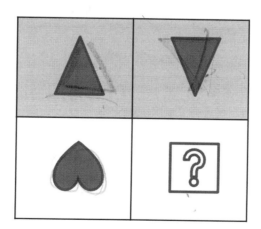

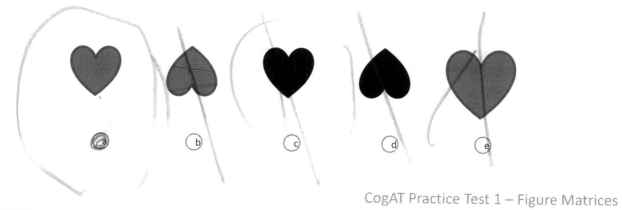

(a)　　　(b)　　　(c)　　　(d)　　　(e)

3.

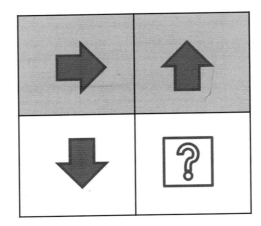

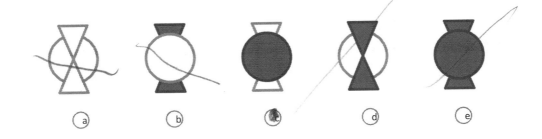

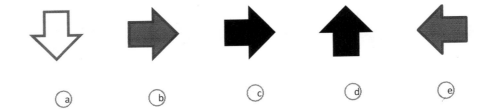

(a)   (b)   (c)   (d)   (e)

4.

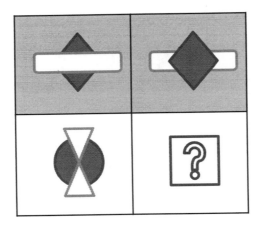

(a)   (b)   (c)   (d)   (e)

5.

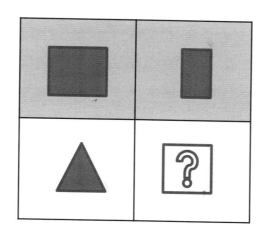

(a)   (b)   (c)   (d)   (e)

6.

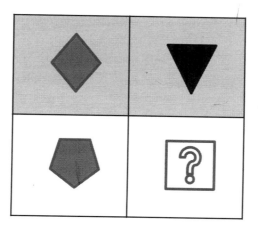

(a)   (b)   (c)   (d)   (e)

7.

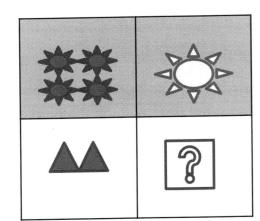

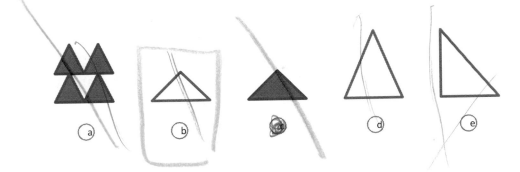

 (a)   (b)   (c) (d) (e)

8.

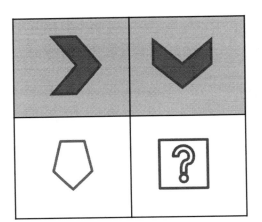

 (a)   (b)   (c)   (d)   (e)

9.

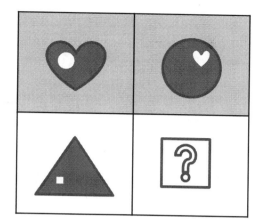

ⓐ   ⓑ   ⓒ   ⓓ   ⓔ

10.

ⓐ   ⓑ   ⓒ   ⓓ   ⓔ

11.

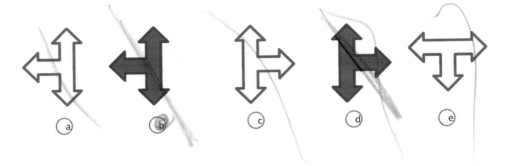

12.

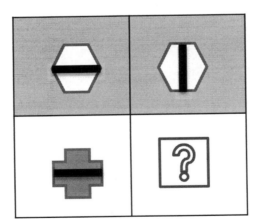

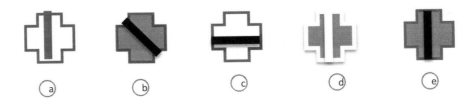

13.

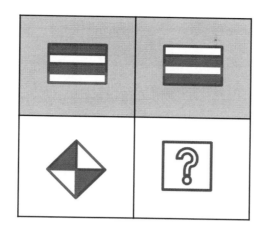

     a   b   c   d   e

14.

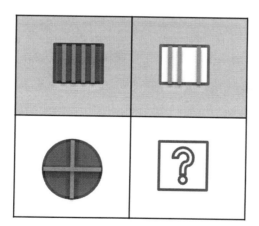

     a   b   c   d   e

15.

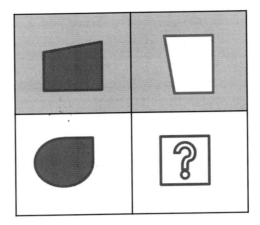

    (a)   (b)   (c)   (d)   (e)

16.

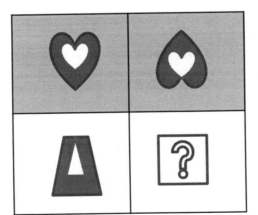

    (a)   (b)   (c)   (d)   (e)

17.

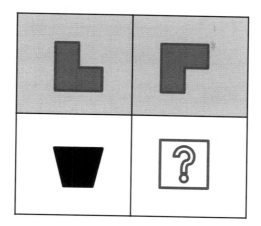

    a   b   c   d   e

18.

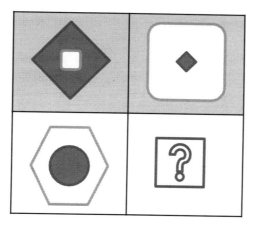

    a   b   c   d   e

PAPER FOLDING

Each question shows a piece of paper that has been folded along the line shown and then has been cut with a pair of scissors or has had holes punched through it.

Pick the answer choice that shows how the paper will look when it is unfolded. Color the bubble under your choice.

1.

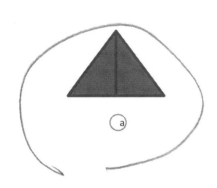

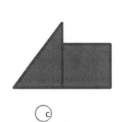

a   b   c

2.

a   b   c

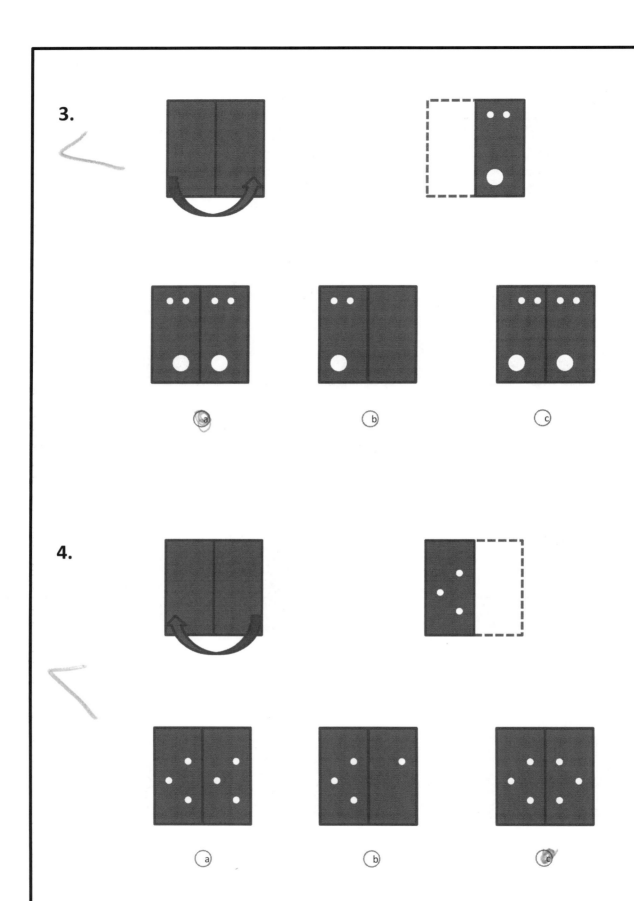

3.

a

b

c

4.

a

b

c

5.

 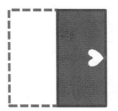

     ⓐ   ⓑ   ⓒ

6.

 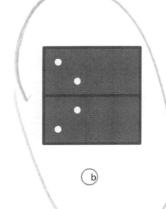 

     ⓐ   ⓑ   ⓒ

7.

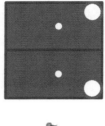  

(a) (b) (c)

8.

(a) (b) (c)

9.

a   b   c

10.

 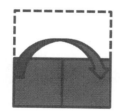 

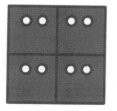  

a   b   c

11.

  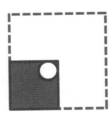

a   b   c

12.

  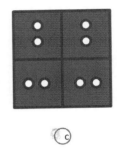

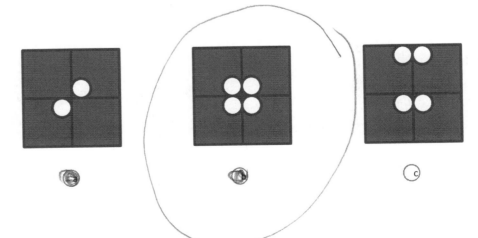

a   b   c

13.

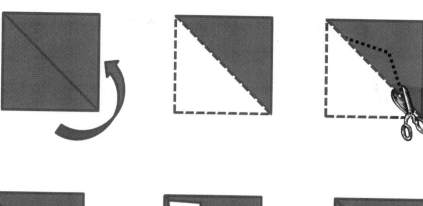

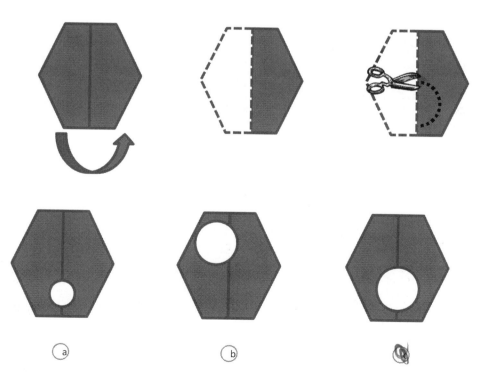

a   b   c

14.

a   b   c

FIGURE CLASSIFICATION

Look at the top 3 pictures and determine how they are similar.

In the bottom row, color the bubble under the picture that is most similar to the top 3.

1.

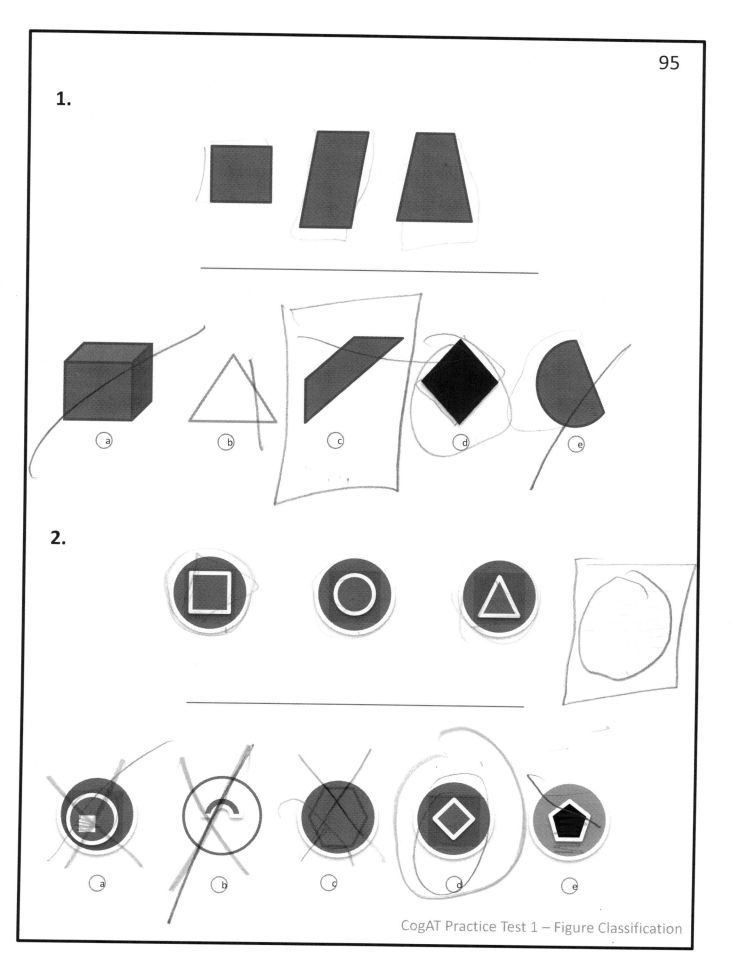

2.

3.

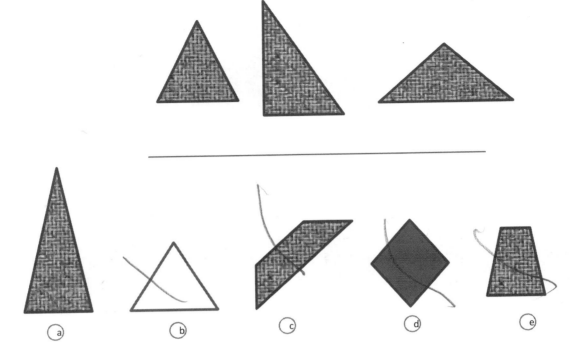

4.

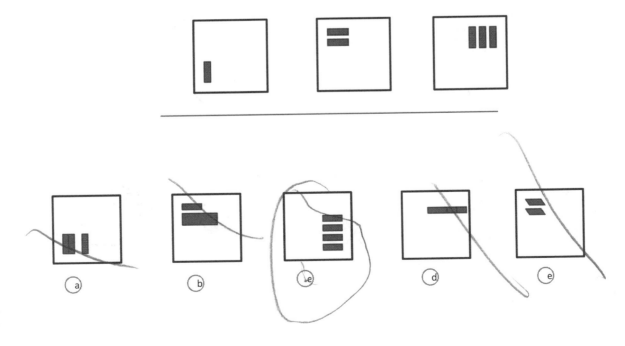

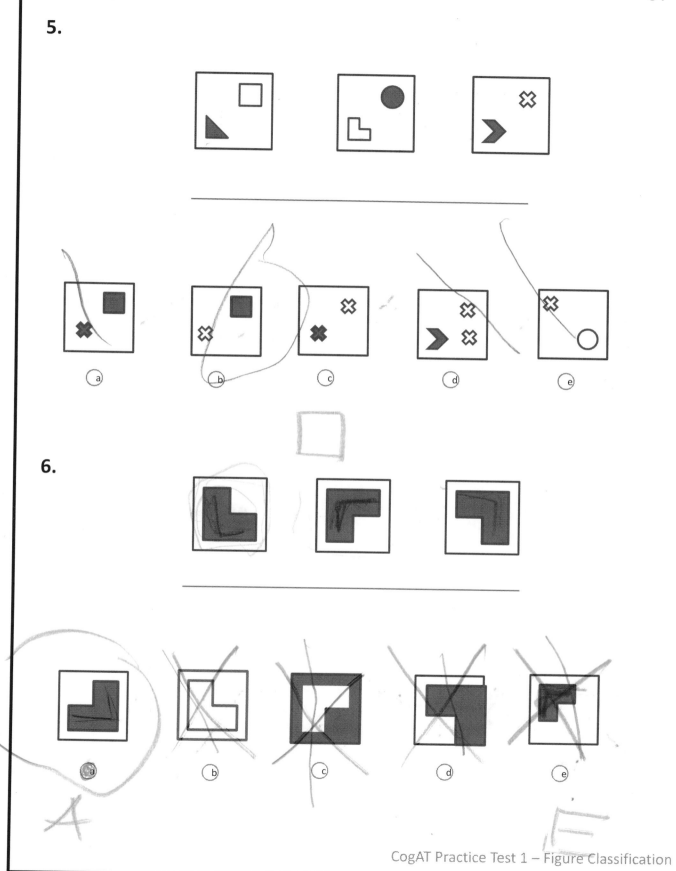

6.

7.

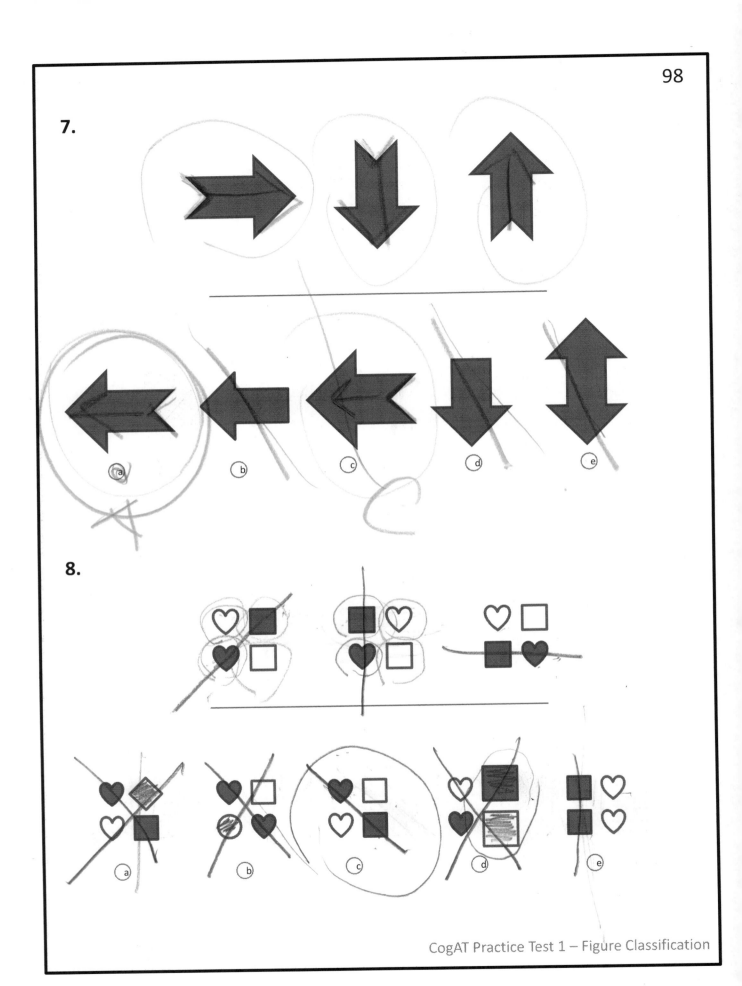

8.

98

9.

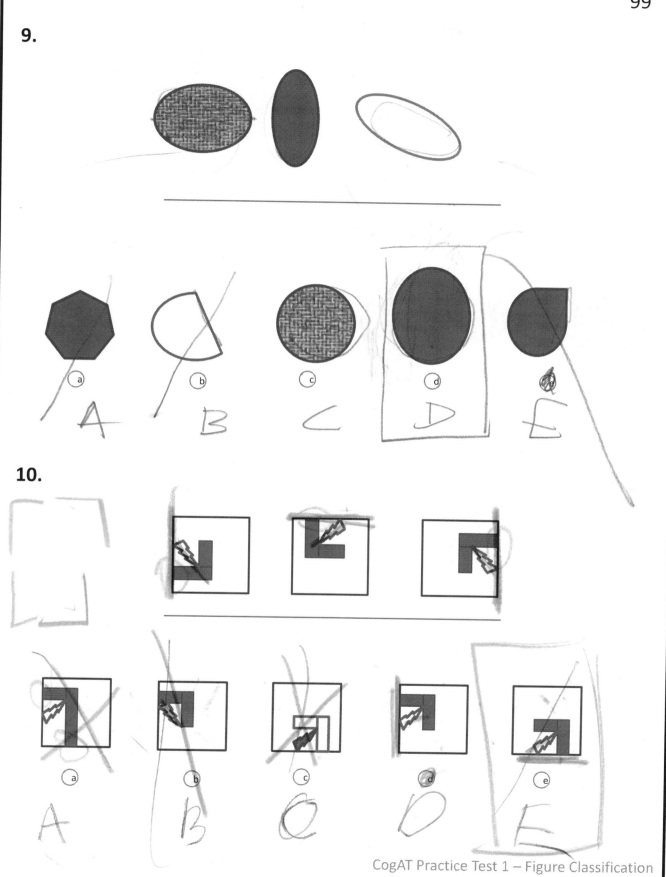

10.

11.

| a | b | c | d | e |

12.

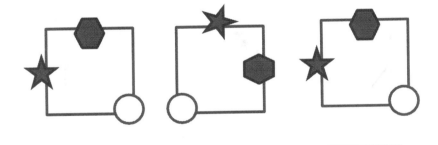

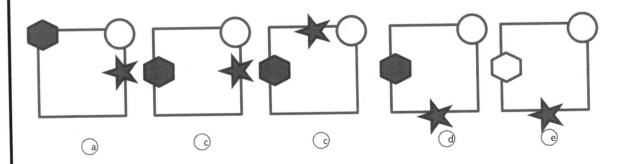

| a | c | c | d | e |

13.

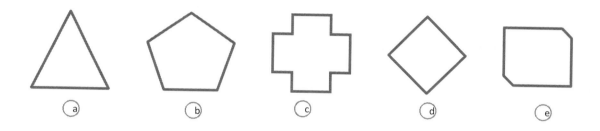

14.

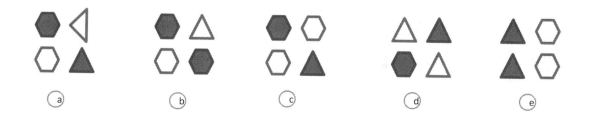

15.

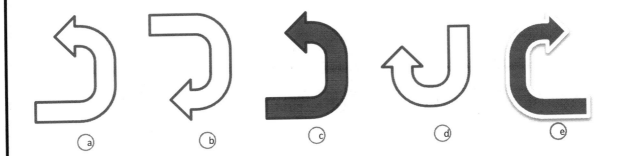

    (a)   (b)   (c)   (d)   (e)

16.

    (a)   (b)   (c)   (d)   (e)

17.

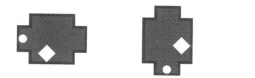

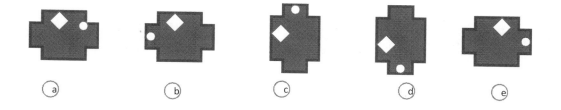

| a | b | c | d | e |

18.

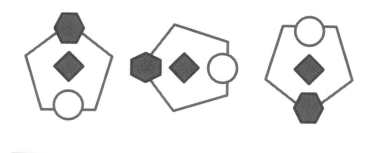

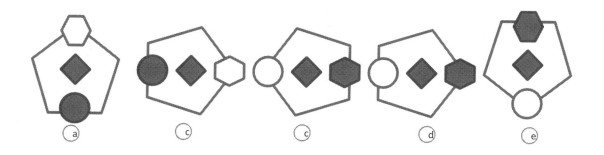

| a | c | c | d | e |

ANSWER KEY

CogAT® PRACTICE TEST 1 – ANSWER KEY

Picture Analogies – *Pg.5 to Pg.15*

1. b
2. c
3. a
4. c
5. a
6. b
7. a
8. c
9. a
10. b
11. b
12. a
13. c
14. b
15. c
16. a
17. c
18. a

CogAT® PRACTICE TEST 1 – ANSWER KEY

Sentence Completion – *Pg.17 to Pg.24*

1. a
2. c
3. b
4. c
5. a
6. c
7. b
8. c
9. c
10. c
11. b
12. c
13. b
14. c
15. a
16. c
17. a
18. b

CogAT® PRACTICE TEST 1 – ANSWER KEY

Picture Classification – *Pg.25 to Pg.35*

1. c
2. b
3. b
4. a
5. c
6. a
7. a
8. b
9. c
10. a
11. c
12. a
13. c
14. a
15. b
16. a
17. c
18. a

CogAT® PRACTICE TEST 1 – ANSWER KEY

Number Analogies – *Pg.37 to Pg.47*

1. a
2. c
3. c
4. c
5. b
6. b
7. a
8. b
9. b
10. a
11. b
12. a
13. c
14. b
15. c
16. a
17. c
18. b

CogAT® PRACTICE TEST 1 – ANSWER KEY

Number Puzzles – *Pg.49 to Pg.57*

1. b
2. c
3. a
4. b
5. a
6. c
7. a
8. b
9. b
10. a
11. c
12. a
13. b
14. c

CogAT® PRACTICE TEST 1 – ANSWER KEY

Number Series – *Pg.59 to Pg.69*

1. b
2. a
3. a
4. c
5. b
6. a
7. b
8. c
9. a
10. b
11. a
12. c
13. b
14. c
15. b
16. a
17. a
18. b

CogAT® PRACTICE TEST 1 – ANSWER KEY

Figure Matrices – *Pg.71 to Pg.81*

1. c
2. a
3. b
4. c
5. a
6. b
7. b
8. d
9. d
10. e
11. a
12. e
13. d
14. c
15. a
16. b
17. a
18. d

CogAT® PRACTICE TEST 1 – ANSWER KEY

Paper Folding – *Pg.83 to Pg.91*

1. a
2. b
3. a
4. c
5. a
6. b
7. a
8. b
9. b
10. b
11. a
12. b
13. a
14. c

CogAT® PRACTICE TEST 1 – ANSWER KEY

Figure Classification – *Pg.93 to Pg.103*

1. c
2. d
3. a
4. c
5. b
6. a
7. a
8. c
9. d
10. e
11. d
12. d
13. d
14. c
15. b
16. b
17. e
18. d

<u>My personal notes</u>

I need to remember to:

I need to watch out for :

FOR ADDITIONAL PRACTICE

Practice Test 2 for the CogAT – Grade 2

FOR ADDITIONAL PRACTICE

Practice Test 2 for the CogAT – Grade 2

Made in the USA
Middletown, DE
18 September 2017